HANDLING A CHILD WITH AUTISM;

Extraordinary guide to help your child defeat and conquer ASD.

Judith K. Adler

Copyright page

Table of contents

Chapter 1

Autism and your child.

Autism Spectrum disorder (ASD) is an issue that influences a kid's sensory system and development and improvement. It frequently appears during a youngster's initial 3 years of life.

A few youngsters with ASD appear to live in their reality. They are not keen on different youngsters and need social mindfulness. A youngster with ASD centers around following a standard that might incorporate typical ways of behaving. A kid with the issue likewise frequently has issues speaking with others. The individual in question may not begin talking when different youngsters. The person probably shouldn't look others in the eyes.

ASD can hold a kid back from creating interactive abilities. This is to some degree because a youngster with ASD will be unable to grasp looks or feelings in others. A youngster with ASD may:

- Not have any desire to be contacted
- Need to play alone
- Not have any desire to change schedules

A youngster with ASD may likewise rehash developments. This may be fluttering their hands or shaking. The person may likewise have strange connections to objects. Yet, a youngster with ASD may likewise do specific mental errands well overall. For instance, the kid might have the option to count or gauge better compared to different youngsters. Youngsters with ASD might do well in craftsmanship or music, or have the memorable option of certain things well overall.

What causes ASD in a kid?

Specialists don't have the foggiest idea of what causes ASD. It could be brought about by specific qualities. A kid with ASD may likewise dislike their cerebrum structure or specific synthetic substances in the mind. Scientists truly do realize that ASD isn't brought about by how a parent brings up a youngster. It is additionally not connected to any immunizations given to youngsters.

Substantially less frequently, different things that might cause ASD to include:

- Being presented to poisons in the climate previously or after birth.

- Extreme contaminations like meningitis or encephalitis that outcome in mind harm.
- Issues during conveyance.
- Contaminations before birth.

Which kids are in danger of ASD?

ASD happens in all racial, ethnic, and financial gatherings. The problem happens substantially more frequently in young men than young ladies. Four to 5 fold the number of young men as young ladies have ASD.

Certain quality issues that disagreement families can bring up a youngster's gamble for ASD. These include:

- Delicate X
- Phenylketonuria (PKU)

- Neurofibromatosis
- Tuberous sclerosis
- Chromosome issues

Your kid might require hereditary testing to take care of find on the off chance that another issue has contributed. The testing is finished by a clinical geneticist. This is a medical care supplier with unique preparation in hereditary qualities and acquired issues. They can tell you the possibility of having one more kid with the quality issue. For instance, PKU conveys a 1 out of 4 possibility of occurring in another pregnancy. For tuberous sclerosis, the odds are 1 out of 2.

In any event, when no quality issue is found, you are at a somewhat higher possibility of having one more kid with ASD. Specialists think this is because a few qualities from the two guardians might act together to cause ASD.

What are the side effects of ASD in a youngster?

Every kid might have a different side effect of ASD. Social side effects include:

- Have issues looking others directly in the eyes.

- Have issues making companions or connecting great with different youngsters.

Correspondence side effects

- Doesn't discuss well with others.

- Begins talking at a later age than different kids or doesn't talk by any means. At the point when the kid can talk, doesn't involve discourse in group environments.

- Rehashes words or expressions (echolalia) or rehashes portions of discourse from TV or films.

- Do rehashed developments, for example, shaking or fluttering fingers or hands.

- Might be excessively delicate or less touchy to specific things around the person in question, like lights, sounds, contact, or taste.

- Has customs.

- Needs schedules.

The side effects of ASD might seem to be other ailments. Ensure your kid sees their medical care supplier for a finding.

How is ASD analyzed in a youngster?

No single clinical trial can analyze ASD. Medical care suppliers utilize specific rules to assist with diagnosing ASD in youngsters before age 2. The rules can assist with diagnosing the issue early. Youngsters determined to have ASD early can be dealt with immediately.

The rules say that all youngsters ought to be evaluated for ASD and other improvement issues before age 2. The screening is finished at well-youngster tests. Youngsters who have side effects of improvement or conduct problems should get more testing for ASD.

- Medical care suppliers search for the accompanying issues during great youngster visits before age 2:

- No jabbering, pointing or signaling by age a year

- No single words were verbally expressed by the age of 16 months

- No 2-word phrases by age two years, simply rehashing words or hints of others

- Loss of any language or interactive abilities at whatever stage in life

- No eye-to-eye connection at 3 to 4 months

If a kid has any of the above issues, the medical care supplier will do a serious screening. This will help show if your youngster has ASD or another formative problem. Your youngster might have to see a medical care supplier with unique preparation to analyze and treat ASD. Your kid may likewise require these screening tests:

- Sensory system test

- Imaging tests, for example, CT output, MRI, or PET sweep

- Emotional wellness tests

- Hereditary tests to search for quality issues that cause ASD or other formative problems

How is ASD treated in a youngster?

Every kid with ASD needs a unique treatment program. This is because kids with ASD can change a great deal in how much assistance they with requiring. Programs that work best are those that are begun as soon as could be expected and incorporate the guardians.

Treatment for ASD incorporates:

- Conduct change programs. These projects show interactive abilities, development abilities, and thinking (mental) abilities. They can assist a kid with changing issue ways of behaving.

- Custom curriculum programs. These emphases on interactive abilities, discourse, language, taking care of oneself, and occupation abilities.

- Medication. A few kids need medication to assist with treating a portion of the side effects of ASD.

Your kid and your family may likewise have to see an emotional well-being supplier. This supplier can give you parent guidance, interactive abilities preparation, and one-on-one treatment. This supplier can likewise assist you with finding the treatment programs that are best for your kid.

Chapter 2

What's ABA to children with autism.

Applied Behavior Analysis (ABA) is a treatment in light of the study of learning and conduct.

Conduct examination assists us with understanding:

- How to conduct functions.
- What conduct is meant for by the climate.
- How learning happens.

ABA treatment applies how we might interpret how conduct functions to genuine circumstances. The objective is to increment ways of behaving that are useful and decline ways of behaving that are unsafe or influence learning.

ABA treatment projects can help:

- Increment language and relational abilities.

- Further develop consideration, center, interactive abilities, memory, and scholastics.

- Decline issue ways of behaving.

The techniques for conducting examinations have been utilized and read up for a long time. They have assisted numerous sorts of students with acquiring various abilities - from better ways of life to learning another dialect. Specialists have utilized ABA to assist youngsters with the mental imbalance and related formative problems since the 1960s.

How does ABA treatment function?

Applied Behavior Analysis includes numerous methods for understanding and evolving conduct. ABA is an adaptable treatment:

- Can be adjusted to address the issues of every special individual.
- Given in a wide range of areas - at home, at school, and locally.
- Instructs abilities that are helpful in day-to-day existence.
- Can include coordinated education or bunch guidance.
- Uplifting feedback.

Uplifting feedback is one of the principal methodologies utilized in ABA.
At the point when a way of behaving is trailed by something esteemed (a prize), an individual is bound to rehash that way of

behaving. After some time, this supports positive conduct change.

To begin with, the specialist distinguishes an objective way of behaving. Each time the individual purposes the way of behaving or expertise effectively, they get a prize. The prize is significant to the individual - models incorporate recognition, a toy or book, watching a video, admittance to a jungle gym or other area, and that's just the beginning.

Positive prizes urge the individual to keep utilizing the ability. Over the long haul, this prompts significant conduct change.

Predecessor, Behavior, Consequence

Figuring out precursors (what occurs before a way of behaving happens) and results (what occurs after the way of behaving) is one more significant piece of any ABA program.

The accompanying three stages - the "A-B-Cs" - help us educate and figure out conduct:

1. A forerunner: this happens just before the objective way of behaving. It very well may be verbal, like an order or solicitation. It can likewise be physical, such as a toy or item, or a light, sound, or something different in the climate. A precursor might come from the climate, from someone else, or be inner (like an idea or feeling).

2. A subsequent way of behaving: this is the individual's reaction or absence of reaction to the predecessor. It tends to be an activity, a verbal reaction, or something different.

3. An outcome: this comes straightforwardly after the way of behaving. It can incorporate encouraging feedback on the ideal way

of behaving, or no response for erroneous/unseemly reactions.

Taking a gander at A-B-Cs assists us with understanding:

Why a way of behaving might occur
What various outcomes could mean for whether the way of behaving is probably going to reoccur?

Model:
Predecessor: The educator says "Now is the right time to tidy up your toys" by the day's end.
Conduct: The understudy shouts "no!"
Result: The instructor eliminates the toys and says "OK, toys are undeniably finished."
What might ABA do for the understudy to gain proficiency with more proper conduct in this present circumstance?

Predecessor: The educator expresses "time to tidy up" by the day's end.

Conduct: The understudy is reminded to inquire, "Might I at any point have 5 additional minutes?"
Outcome: The instructor says, "obviously you can have 5 additional minutes!"
With proceeding with training, the understudy will want to supplant the improper way of behaving with a more useful one. This is a simpler way for the understudy to fulfill the kid's requirements!

What Does an ABA Program Involve?

Great ABA programs for chemical imbalance are not "one size fits all." ABA ought not to be seen as a canned arrangement of drills. Rather, each program is composed to address the issues of the singular student.

The objective of any ABA program is to assist every individual with chipping away at abilities that will assist them with turning out to be more free and fruitful in the present moment as well as from here on out.

Arranging and Ongoing Assessment

A certified and prepared conduct examiner (BCBA) plans and straightforwardly regulates the program. They modify the ABA program to every student's abilities, needs, interests, inclinations, and family circumstances.

The BCBA will begin by doing an itemized evaluation of every individual's abilities and inclinations. They will utilize this to compose explicit treatment objectives. Family objectives and inclinations might be incorporated, as well.

Treatment objectives are composed because of the age and capacity level of the individual with ASD. Objectives can incorporate a wide range of expertise regions, for example,

- Correspondence and language.
- Interactive abilities.
- Taking care of oneself, (for example, showering, and toileting)
- Play and relaxation
- Coordinated abilities.
- Mastering and scholastic abilities.

The guidance plan separates every one of these abilities into little, substantial advances. The specialist shows each stage individually, from basic (for example mimicking single sounds) to more perplexing (for example carrying on a discussion).

The BCBA and advisors measure progress by gathering information in every treatment meeting. The information assists them with checking the individual's advancement toward objectives on a continuous premise.

The conduct investigator routinely meets with relatives and program staff to survey data about progress. They can then prepare and change showing plans and objectives depending on the situation.

ABA Techniques and Philosophy

The educator utilizes an assortment of ABA methodology. Some are coordinated by the teacher and others are coordinated by the individual with mental imbalance.

Guardians, relatives, and parental figures get prepared so they can uphold mastering and ability to practice over the day.

The individual with mental imbalance will have numerous chances to acquire and rehearse abilities every day. This can occur in both arranged and normally happening circumstances. For example, somebody figuring out how to welcome others by saying "hi" may be able to rehearse this ability in the study hall with their educator (arranged) and on the jungle gym during a break (normally happening).

The student gets an overflow of uplifting feedback for exhibiting helpful abilities and socially proper ways of behaving. The accentuation is on certain social associations and agreeable learning.

The student gets no support for ways of behaving that posture hurt or forestall learning.

ABA is powerful for individuals, all things considered. It tends to be utilized from youth through adulthood!

Who provides ABA services?

A board-guaranteed conduct investigator (BCBA) gives ABA treatment administrations. To turn into a BCBA, coming up next is required:

- Procure a graduate degree or Ph.D. in brain research or conduct an examination.
- Breeze through a public certificate test.
- Look for a state permit to rehearse. (in certain states)

ABA treatment programs additionally include advisors, or enlisted conduct professionals (RBTs). These advisors are prepared and managed by the BCBA. They work straightforwardly with youngsters and grown-ups with a chemical imbalance to rehearse abilities and work toward the singular objectives composed by the BCBA. You might hear them alluded to by at least a couple of names: conduct specialists, line advisors, conduct tech, and so forth.

What is the proof that ABA works?

ABA is viewed as a proof-based best practice treatment by the US Surgeon General and by the American Psychological Association.

"Proof based" implies that ABA has breezed through logical assessments of its convenience, quality, and adequacy. ABA treatment incorporates a wide range of methods. These strategies center around forerunners (what occurs before a way of behaving happens) and on results (what occurs after the way of behaving).

More than 20 examinations have laid out that concentrated and long-haul treatment utilizing ABA standards further develops results for the majority however not all kids with mental imbalance. "Serious" and "long haul" allude to programs that give 25 to 40 hours every seven days of treatment for 1 to 3 years. These examinations show acquires in scholarly working, language improvement, everyday living abilities, and social working. Studies with grown-ups utilizing ABA standards, however less in number, show comparative advantages.

Is ABA covered by insurance?

Once in a while. Many kinds of private health care coverage are expected to cover ABA administrations. This relies upon what sort of protection you have, and what state you live in.

All Medicaid plans should cover therapies that are restoratively important for kids younger than 21. If a specialist endorses ABA and says it is restoratively fundamental for your youngster, Medicaid should take care of the expense.

You can likewise contact the Autism Response Team assuming you experience issues getting inclusion, or need extra assistance.

Where do I find ABA administrations?
To get everything rolling, follow these means:

Talk with your pediatrician or other clinical suppliers about ABA. They can talk about whether ABA is appropriate for your youngster. They can compose a solution for ABA if it is fundamental for your protection.

Check whether your insurance agency takes care of the expense of ABA treatment, and what your advantage is.

Scan asset catalog for ABA suppliers close to you. Or then again, ask your youngster's primary care physician and educators for suggestions.

Call the ABA supplier and solicitation an admission assessment. Have a few inquiries prepared (see underneath!)

What inquiries would it be a good idea for me to pose?

It's critical to find an ABA supplier and specialists who are ideal for your loved ones. The initial step is for specialists to lay out a decent connection with your youngster. If your youngster confides in his advisors and appreciates investing energy with them, treatment will find success - and fun!

The accompanying inquiries can assist you with assessing whether a supplier will be ideal for your loved ones. Make sure to pay attention to your gut feelings, also!

- What number of BCBAs do you have on staff?

- Might it be said that they are authorized with the BACB and through the state?

- What number of social specialists do you have?

- What number of specialists will be working with my kid?

- What kind of preparation do your specialists get? How frequently?

- How much direct management do specialists get from BCBAs week after week?

- How would you oversee security concerns?

- What does a commonplace ABA meeting resemble?
- Do you offer locally established or center-based treatment?
- How would you decide objectives for my kid?
- What do you think about input from guardians?
- How frequently do you rethink objectives?
- How is progress assessed?
- How long each week could you at any point give?
- Do you have a standby list?
- What kind of insurance do you acknowledge?

4 Ways ABA Can Help My Child with Autism.

Applied Behavior Analysis (ABA) is broadly perceived as the best treatment for people with mental imbalance. ABA treatment is a discipline given to the comprehension and improvement of the human way of behaving, zeroing in on equitably characterized, discernible ways of behaving of social importance. ABA uses numerous encouraging feedback techniques to work on different abilities.

ABA is not a one-size-fits-all methodology. ABA projects ought to continuously be explicitly individualized for your kid and their requirements, learning style, favored things, and so on. Appraisals are continually reconsidered to guarantee that your kid's necessities are met.

There are numerous ways that ABA can assist your youngster with a mental imbalance, including the four central issues illustrated underneath:

1. Work on Social Skills.

One of the most pervasive difficulties for people with mental imbalance range jumble is in the space of interactive abilities. These incorporate subjects, for example, observational abilities, eye-to-eye connection, play collaborations, social pragmatics, sharing pleasure, and building connections.

Interactive abilities programs assist youngsters with building connections and effectively exploring different social circumstances while having a positive social companion insight.

Another way that interactive abilities can be improved is through Speech Therapy. High mountain teams up with your neighborhood

Speech Pathologist to cultivate consistency and increment your kid's capacity to utilize mastered abilities across conditions and people. Language training can help youngsters with communicating their needs and needs (verbally and nonverbally), assisting them with grasping words and bearings and making them all the more effortlessly perceived by others in a customary verbal climate.

ABA can assist kids with chemical imbalances learn and distinguishing how to make associations with others and at last cultivate associations with companions, friends, and relatives.

2. Further, develop Effective Parenting Skills.

It has been demonstrated that guardians who are effectively engaged with their youngster's treatment frequently see greater improvement in their kids. Our clinical group is prepared to fabricate conduct designs that help the whole nuclear family. Our family-focused treatment model coordinates parental figures at all stages, including objective choice, program execution, and progress appraisal. We guide you to incorporate learning through play and normal schedules, so it doesn't feel like "schoolwork," which thus builds maintenance of learned ways of behaving.

In understanding the ABA procedures utilized by your Board Certified Behavior Analysis (BCBA), executing them in your day-to-day schedules, and building up their learnings, your connections with your youngster will be more successful and purposeful. It will likewise assist your kid in withholding the data learned and figuring out the communications as typical. By being effectively engaged with your kid's arrangement, you'll figure out how to take special care of their interesting requirements and assist with arriving at their formative objectives.

3. Work on Living Skills and Encourage Independence.

A youngster's day is comprised of exercises and schedules. These exercises and schedules can incorporate playing with toys, getting dressed, utilizing utensils during feasts, or following bearings. These exercises are fundamental for a youngster's turn of events. One more type of treatment utilized for people with mental imbalance is Occupational Therapy. Snow-capped mountain moreover teams up with your neighborhood Occupational Therapist to cultivate consistency and increment your kid's capacity to utilizc acquired abilities across conditions and people. Word-related treatment assists youngsters with fostering these abilities.

Chemical imbalance disorder and your kid.

Word related Therapy can likewise assist kids with growing fine coordinated movements by working on their capacity to handle and deliver toys and increment the smoothness of their fingers. This may likewise incorporate progressing pre-endlessly penmanship abilities.

Recognizing and tending to take care of oneself deferrals like washing, dressing, cleaning teeth, and taking care of oneself is a basic piece of improvement also. Large numbers of these assignments frequently require strength in the hands, fingers, and chest area. Word-related treatment will attempt to fortify these muscles to further develop the simplicity and feasibility of these everyday capabilities.

By fostering these fundamental taking care of oneself undertakings and making maintainable schedules, kids with mental imbalance can steadily turn out to be more autonomous.

4. Work on Overall Quality of Life.

I maintain that your kid should be all that they can be in a complicated existence where meaningful gestures can be difficult to peruse, in any event, for the best of us.
I accept it is vital to assist kids with genuine circumstances, in actuality, places, to participate in this great world we as a whole offer.

By having an individualized educational plan, your kid will be set up to succeed and develop personally. You'll have the option to see the improvement and upgrades that your kid has made and at last watch, they arrive at even the most troublesome objectives and achievements. ABA is intended to assist your youngster with arriving at their maximum capacity and carrying on with their most ideal life while being their actual selves.

Applied Behavior Analysis is the most explored and compelling treatment for youngsters with a mental imbalance range jumble. At the point when utilized as an early mediation strategy, ABA projects can incorporate more chances to assist kids with chemical imbalances better take part on the planet.

Chapter 3

Understanding his/her communication

Youngsters with ASD experience difficulty connecting with others. They experience difficulty visually connecting. They frequently pull out into themselves. They might appear to be uninterested in connecting with relatives.

However, a few youngsters with ASD might very much want to continue to chat with relatives, companions, and even outsiders about a point they are fixated on. The issue is that they might discuss it excessively lengthy. Or on the other hand, they might discuss that one subject. This can drive others away.

If you are a parent or grandparent of a kid with ASD, it very well may be unfortunate on the off chance that you feel like you can't associate with them. In any case, getting more familiar with these issues and what has helped other people can help you and your relationship.

Getting through the hindrances of ASD

ASD has no fix. Be that as it may, there is trust through treatment. Numerous kids can figure out how to convey and communicate. Medical care suppliers and emotional well-being specialists have gleaned some significant knowledge about how to get through to these kids.

Here are a few things I am familiar with kids with an ASD:

- They will be unable to grasp your nonverbal interchanges. They may not respond to your grin or grimace.

- They take things in a real sense. You should be mindful to say the preciseness exact thing you mean. If you rush the kid by expressing "Step on it," don't be shocked assuming they request that what step on.

- They may simply have the option to deal with each thought or thought in turn. Keep discussions engaged and basic.

- They probably will need to just discuss the one thing they are truly intrigued by at a given time. Also, they might need to discuss it again and again.

- They might see things uniquely in contrast to what you do. You may not see conventional sounds, tastes, contacts, scents, and sights. However, these might be genuinely difficult for the kid.

Correspondence and association tips for ASD.

For a good explanation, families, educators, and others need to know how they can advance language improvement in nonverbal kids or teens with mental imbalance. Fortunately, research has delivered various viable techniques.

In any case, before I share my "top tips," it's memorable's critical that every individual with chemical imbalance is novel. Indeed, even with enormous exertion, a system that functions admirably with one youngster or teen may not work with another. And, surprisingly, however every individual with mental imbalance can figure out how to impart, but it's not generally through communication in the language. Nonverbal people with mental imbalance have a lot to add to society and can live satisfying lives with the assistance of visual backings and assistive innovations.

There are no immovable guidelines on the best way to speak with a youngster with ASD. Yet, numerous relatives have had accomplishments with these tips:

1. Show restraint.

It frequently takes a kid with ASD longer to handle data. You might have to dial back your discussion to their speed. Long stops can be useful.

Show the kid how to communicate outrage without being excessively forceful. Kids with ASD ought to realize that they don't need to hold their annoyance and disappointment inside.

2. Be relentless yet versatile.

Try not to allow your sentiments to get injured if the kid doesn't answer you as you'd like. Youngsters with ASD might have inconvenience in both appearance and controlling their feelings. They can be gruff in their reactions. Try not to think about this literally.

3. Continuously stay positive.

Youngsters with ASD answer best to uplifting feedback. Make certain to discuss or compensate for appropriate conduct frequently. Be liberal with praises for a good way of behaving.

4. Disregard disturbing alluring way of behaving.

A kid with ASD might act horribly on occasion to inspire you to zero in on them. Overlooking this conduct is many times the most effective way to forestall it. Likewise, discuss and remunerate the kid's appropriate conduct frequently.

5. Collaborate through active work.

Kids with ASD will more often than not definitely stand out ranges. This is particularly obvious with regards to imparting. Going around and playing outside might be a superior approach to sharing time. It will likewise allow them to unwind and feel more settled.

6. Be warm and aware.

Youngsters with ASD frequently need an embrace, very much like different kids. Here and there they need this substantially more than different kids. However, a few youngsters could do without being contacted by any means, even light contact can trouble them. Regard their own space. Never force actual fondness on a reluctant kid.

7. Show your adoration and interest. Youngsters with ASD might experience difficulty showing their sentiments. Yet, they need to realize that you love them. Make a special effort to communicate your advantage, be mindful, and support.

8. Gain from your youngster.

Your kid's extraordinary needs and capacities might show you a method for taking a gander at the world that you won't ever consider. As troublesome as it could be on certain days, unwinding, chuckling, and partaking in the special gift that is your kid can furnish both you and your family with many prizes.

9. Accept.

A youngster with ASD is most importantly a kid. They are a developing individual with obscure potential outcomes. Trust in what the youngster can do. Try not to characterize the youngster by a determination.

10. Deal with yourself.

Enjoying some time off is OK. Join parent support gatherings. Or on the other hand, ask understanding loved ones to focus on your kid so you can re-energize. School analysts and guides can likewise give assets to help you.

It very well may be trying to communicate with a youngster or grandkid with ASD. Yet, it's perhaps of the main thing you can do to assist that kid with learning. Research shows that early, continuous, and adoring association of relatives is one of the most amazing ways of assisting kids with ASD.

These tips underneath have shown to be truly useful as well.

Support play and social cooperation.

Kids learn through play, and that incorporates learning a language. Intelligent play gives agreeable open doors to you and your kid to impart.

Attempt different games to find those your kid appreciates. Additionally, attempt fun-loving exercises that advance the social association.
Models incorporate singing, recounting nursery rhymes, and delicate roughhousing.

During your cooperation, position yourself before your kid and near eye level - so it's simpler for your kid to see and hear you.

Copy your youngster. Copying your youngster's sounds and play ways of behaving will energize expression and collaboration. It additionally urges your kid to duplicate you and alternate. Ensure you emulate how your kid is playing - since it's a positive way of behaving. For instance, when your kid moves a vehicle, you roll a vehicle. Assuming that the person crashes the vehicle, you crash yours as well. However, don't copy tossing the vehicle!

Center around nonverbal correspondence.

Motions and eye-to-eye connections can construct an establishment for language. Support your youngster by displaying and answering these ways of behaving. Overstate your motions. Utilize both your body and your voice while conveying - for instance, by stretching out your hand to the moment that you say "look" and gesturing your head when you say "OK." Use motions that are simple for your kid to copy. Models incorporate applauding, opening hands, connecting arms, and so forth.

Answer your youngster's motions.

Whenever she checks out or focuses on a toy, hand it to her or take the prompt for you to play with it. Likewise, highlight a toy you need before getting it.
Leave "space" for your kid to talk. It's normal to want to fill in language when a kid doesn't quickly answer. Yet, it's so critical to offer your youngster bunches of chances to impart, regardless of whether he isn't talking. At the point when you pose an inquiry or see that your kid needs something, stop for a few seconds while taking a gander at him hopefully. Watch for any sound or body development and answer speedily. The quickness of your reaction

assists your kid with feeling the force of correspondence.

Improve your language.

Doing so assists your kid with following what you're talking about. It additionally makes it more straightforward for her to mimic your discourse. Assuming your youngster is nonverbal, have a go at talking generally in single words. (If she's playing with a ball, you say "ball" or "roll.") If your kid is talking single words, raise the stakes. Talk in short expressions, for example, "roll ball" or "toss ball." Keep following this "one-up" rule: Generally use phrases with another word than your kid is utilizing.

Autism and correspondence:

Will my nonverbal kid ever speak? Follow your kid's advantages. As opposed to intruding on your youngster's concentration, track with words. Utilizing the one-up rule, describe what your youngster is doing. If he's playing with a shape sorter, you could give the signal "in" when he places a shape in its space. You could say "shape" when he holds up the shape and "dump shapes" when he dumps them out to begin once again. By discussing what connects with your youngster, you'll assist him with learning the related jargon.

Think about assistive gadgets and visual backings.

Assistive innovations and visual backings can accomplish more than replace discourse. They can cultivate its turn of events. Models incorporate gadgets and applications with pictures that your kid contacts to create words. On a more straightforward level, visual backings can incorporate pictures and gatherings of pictures that your kid can use to demonstrate solicitations and contemplations.

Chapter 4

Disciplining alternatives for children with autism.

At the point when a kid gets into mischief, whether the dangerous way of behaving is pitching an attitude fit, hitting another youngster, or disregarding directions, you might be leaned to reprove them or remove specific honors. Be that as it may, training a youngster with chemical imbalance might require an alternate methodology.

For what reason do youngsters with mental imbalance require rules and discipline?
Limits are vital to living in the public eye, regardless of your neurological cosmetics. Like all kids – however maybe to a more noteworthy degree than most – youngsters with chemical imbalance normally blossom with a schedule. Laying out rules and cutoff points is an approach to supporting

schedules, which might be a solace to messes with mental imbalance.

Conventional discipline methods aren't generally viable for a kid with a chemical imbalance. Contingent upon where they fall on the range, they could battle to grasp results or handle brutal censures. However, that doesn't mean you shouldn't utilize any discipline whatsoever. All things considered, gentler and predictable systems might be the way to assist youngsters with chemical imbalances and deal with their way of behaving.

Step-by-step instructions to Manage Misbehavior Without Punishment.

Grasping Common Autistic Behaviors.
We generally discipline youngsters since they deliberately act in improper ways, whether it's swiping treats off a kin's plate or purposefully stumbling a kid on the soccer field. Nonetheless, a kid with a chemical

imbalance will most likely be unable to control specific ways of behaving, and they mustn't be cruelly rebuffed for them. Ways of behaving that youngsters with ASD might battle to control include:

- Gnawing their hands and fingers.
- Hand fluttering or shaking (a self-invigorating way of behaving that assists individuals with chemical imbalance control their feelings)
- Shouting or hollering.
- Harming themselves by banging or hitting their heads.
- Not taking a gander at individuals or visually connecting.
- Actual hostility toward peers and adults, such as gnawing or kicking.

Large numbers of these ways of behaving stem from kids' battles to communicate their requirements or wants or figure out accepted practices and cues.1 You shouldn't put your kid on a break, disgrace them, or hit them given these ways of behaving. Rather, it's significant you work to more readily comprehend the reason why they are carrying on along these lines and, if fundamental, attempt to keep away from those triggers from now on.

Utilize Positive Reinforcement.

Youngsters with mental imbalance answer better to teach procedures that emphasize the positive. With uplifting feedback systems, you point out things your kid is doing well (involving their tranquil voice in the general store, for instance) and applaud them or award them for it.

A few youngsters may be propelled by an exemplary sticker diagram, where they can gather stickers for a good way of behaving and in the long run procure an award for a specific number of stickers.

However, numerous kids with a chemical imbalance, especially youthful ones, answer more prompt positive input and rewards that relate straightforwardly to the way of behaving. For instance, on the off chance that they ask pleasantly for a squishy toy in a store as opposed to shouting or hitting their heads in dissatisfaction, they procure prompt recognition (and perhaps, if suitable, the toy).

How Praise Can Promote Good Behavior.

Show Self-Calming Techniques.
Implosions are normal in kids, yet it can become more enthusiastically to quiet a youngster with a chemical imbalance. A few youngsters with mental imbalance can learn self-quieting strategies for when they begin

to feel crazy about themselves or a circumstance.

One basic self-quieting strategy they can attempt is to take in and out through their nose gradually while shutting their eyes and envisioning something charming, similar to their kitty or their number one park. Assuming that you or one more believed grown-up is near, they can embrace the grown-up until they're settled. Delicate, consistent tension, as from an embrace, is quieting for some youngsters with autism.3

Control Their Environment.

For youngsters with chemical imbalance particularly, it's useful to make their quick climate helpful for their solace. Taking consideration filling their play region or room with favored toys and items can cause them to have a solid sense of security and agreeable, which might prompt more controlled conduct.

Alternately, attempt to stay away from circumstances that you know can set off their fomentation — for certain children with a chemical imbalance, for instance, it very well may be packed or loud puts — and be keeping watch for indications of forthcoming dissatisfaction. In some cases, messes with chemical imbalance can be habitual about certain toys or exercises and that can impede essential routines.1 These interruptions can be eliminated when undertakings should be finished.

Stick to Routines.

Many children with chemical imbalance hunger for consistency and request and can battle to adapt when standard schedules are disrupted.2 They could become suddenly angry or increment self-invigorating ways of behaving to manage erratic circumstances. Assist them by restricting the number of exercises you with having them do and adhering to an anticipated timetable.

That could mean skirting a language training meeting multi-week as opposed to knocking it to one more day when the educator is unintentionally twofold reserved or making an effort not to fit in abrupt, surprising tasks with them following some serious time school. Make a timetable that you can show in your kid's room or a typical region with pictures they can use to rapidly recognize what they can hope to do every day of the week (like a photograph of their language teacher on Tuesday).

Impart Clearly.

It's ideal to utilize plain language and orders with kids who have a mental imbalance. Kids with mental imbalance range problems frequently experience difficulty grasping nuances in verbal language or non-verbal communication.

At the point when your kid begins carrying on, direct them to what you favor them to do instead of what they shouldn't do. For instance, if a kid is pulling a canine's tail, don't say, "Quit harming the canine." Instead, you can say, "Pet the canine delicately."

Overlook Harmless Behaviors.

A few ways of behaving of youngsters with mental imbalance appear to be odd however aren't risky or troublesome. Essential instances of this are self-animating ways of behaving like hand-fluttering or shaking.

If issue conduct happens rarely, doesn't keep your family or others from customary schedules, and doesn't hurt your kid or others, then it ought to be overlooked whenever the situation allows.

Put Safety First.

Numerous kids with mental imbalance don't show conduct that would hurt themselves or others. In any case, at whatever point you are managing a conduct circumstance where a kid is truly suddenly erupting, you want to ensure that they (and others around them) are protected.

Assuming your youngster is having a fit that is difficult to stop, make certain to eliminate hard or sharp items that may be in their way. If you are experiencing difficulty eliminating your kid from a populated spot, (for example, the jungle gym or a birthday celebration), select assistance from one more adult to occupy and guide different youngsters to another area.

Look for Professional Help.

Assuming you are finding it hard to deal with your kid's way of behaving, feel free to proficient assistance. Search for individuals with aptitude in assisting youngsters with a chemical imbalance, as formative conduct pediatricians or kid clinicians.

There are a few treatments that have been demonstrated to be useful for youngsters with a chemical imbalance. Most originate from the standards of applied conduct investigation (ABA) made sense of the above which centers around building and empowering new abilities, giving admittance to favored exercises and toys, giving children decisions while conceivable, expanding proper correspondence, and making complex circumstances more unsurprising utilizing signals and other routine motions.

Significantly, you work with your kid's school to lay out a common way to deal with discipline. Having comparative assumptions and methodologies will permit youngsters to extend examples gained from school to home, as well as the other way around.

It's difficult to bring up a kid with chemical imbalance (or any kid, besides), however, it's critical to realize that they are not carrying on to be terrible or to challenge you. They are generally attempting to convey or manage profoundly awkward sentiments. They merit care and empathy, never cruel or actual discipline.

To assist with advancing appropriate conduct in a youngster with a chemical imbalance, stay with unsurprising circumstances and settings, express your desires obviously and straightforwardly, and practice persistence when certain ways of behaving may appear to be odd yet aren't risky. What's more, when a circumstance appears to be too hard to even consider dealing with, don't be hesitant to look for help from clinical experts who can support and guide you.

Chapter 5

Home and academic activities for your child with autism.

Since around 1 out of 59 Autistic kids is determined to have a chemical imbalance, figuring out how to assist Autistic kids with this problem in the home and study hall is so significant.

Showing youthful understudies with chemical imbalance relational abilities and learning systems makes it all almost certain that they'll arrive at their scholarly potential later on. Furthermore, the more you find out about chemical imbalance range jumble, the better you'll have the option to set up these understudies for long-lasting achievement.

These are phenomenal ways of keeping understudies with mental imbalance drawn in and prepared to learn.

Great action can be a useful asset for assisting youngsters with a mental imbalance to explore their surroundings. I have ordered a rundown of our 5 most loved exercises. You may currently know all about them, yet underneath I have framed a few thoughts on the most proficient method to transform these thoughts into growth opportunities, from working on interactive abilities and correspondence to dealing with feelings and faculties.

Exercises at home.

1. Songs.

Music and melodies offer youngsters with chemical imbalances an elective approach to communicating feelings and learning. Many guardians review the letter set by rapidly singing the "letters in order melody," which has been implanted in our recollections since adolescence.

In this vein, tunes are particularly helpful for "workable minutes." Does your kid have an everyday practice toward the beginning of the day? It's not difficult to concoct a tune (although YouTube probably has a few suggestions) for covering every one of the things in your daily schedule. Pick a melody that your youngster would be able "murmur" while cleaning their teeth. Perhaps a tune to sing while at the same time tidying up after recess? You can likewise incorporate development into melodies and music, such as moving, tapping, or drumming to rehearse coordinated abilities, body mindfulness, and add active work.

2. I Spy.

An exemplary game can truly show some signs of life for guardians and their kids with autism. Since people with mental imbalance frequently battle with portrayals, especially putting various types of descriptors together, I Spy is an ideal answer for training. (Furthermore, it costs nothing!) The conventional situation can be played among guardians and kids involving regular things in your home or when you are making the rounds (it's an extraordinary game to play if you maintain that your kid should center). I Spy can be customized as well. For kids with handling hardships, take a stab at restricting the item choices to only 2 or 3 and have your kid pick the right one. You can likewise involve it as a method for rehearsing explicit jargon by restricting depictions to varieties or shapes.

3. Manikins.

As a general rule, kids love manikins. This is extraordinary news since manikins permit guardians to integrate workable minutes into fun play. Offering viewpoints and managing feelings are overwhelming assignments for kids, especially for youngsters with autism. Frequently it is more straightforward for youngsters to put themselves out there if they do it through an "outsider" like a manikin. Besides involving manikins in this open limit, they can likewise be utilized for training pretend to deal with interactive abilities and being in new conditions. Guardians find them valuable before groundbreaking occasions like going to another everyday schedule; along these lines, you can manage what's in store employing the manikins, which ideally reduces a portion of the uneasiness ahead of time. For added imaginative tomfoolery, make your manikins.

Play-Doh/Air-Dry Clay/Moon Sand.

Another youth staple, Play-Doh (and different varieties) permits you and your kid to make pretty much anything. These different "batters" are particularly useful for youngsters with tactile issues since they are pliant, squeezable, and come in many tones. While you can make figures, tea sets, winged serpents, or whatever else your kid's heart wants, Play-Doh can likewise be a helpful showing instrument (work on making numbers or letter set letters). Moon Sand is a famous new choice to Play-Doh that offers a more tangible encounter since it is grainier, simpler to push through, and enjoyable to hold. Since it's not quite so intense as Play-Doh, it's a magnificent choice for youngsters with restricted fine engine capability. You likewise don't need to spend a fortune on it.

4. Otsimo.

Otsimo's free instructive games are a simple method for getting your youngster to learn in various ways. While managing Otsimo's huge list of games, your youngster is additionally rehearsing fine engine developments and concentration. There are many motivations behind why Otsimo stands apart from other custom curriculum applications, yet the primary explanation individuals probably notice is that it is free.

While there is an exceptional rendition accessible utilizing membership, Otsimo's base application (with more than 50 games, an AAC correspondence capability, progress following for guardians, and individualized instruction through their particular calculation) is accessible at no expense and without any promotions.

Otsimo likewise covers a ton of domains. The games educate and build up new material by drawing on various learning styles and consolidating multi-tangible improvements. Find creatures and the sounds they make. Do jigsaw riddles (or even better, make your own!). Investigating day-to-day existence points, similar to colors, climate, feelings, and food, alongside numerous others is never an errand because Otsimo approaches training according to the viewpoint of having a good time. It's a multi-capability application that develops with your youngster and permits them to, freely, find the magnificence in learning.

5. Name Game

This tomfoolery bunch correspondence action shows understudies with mental imbalance a fundamental ability: how to present themselves and learn another person's name. To play this game, assemble your understudies all around so they can all see one another. Begin by pointing at yourself and saying your name ("I am Mr. or Ms. ______."). Then, ask the kid to your right side to share their name very much as you did and afterward rehash your name while pointing at you. Have every youngster take a turn saying their name, then, at that point, pointing at one more kid in the class and rehashing their name.

The Name Game is a particularly fun interactive abilities movement for youngsters with autism to do toward the start of the school year. Like that, they'll have the option to get familiar with their schoolmates' names and get an early advantage on making new companions.

SCHOOL exercises.

1. Storytime at Nursery.

"How Would It Feel to Be ____?"
Next time you read a book to your group, have a go at asking your understudies how it would feel to be the principal character in the story. If you're perusing an image book about Cinderella, for instance, you could ask how they would feel assuming that they had two underhanded stepsisters who consistently treated them badly. Or on the other hand, if you're perusing Peter Pan as a class, you could ask them what cheerful recollections they would think going to fly with enchantment pixie dust.

This can assist understudies with mental imbalance learn sympathy as well as how to see circumstances in their lives according to another point of view. It can likewise show them how to perceive close-to-home signs by empowering them to place themselves in the viewpoint of someone else.

2. Sharing Time

Sharing time is an exemplary grade school staple, and it can likewise be an extraordinary social-profound learning (SEL) movement for youngsters with mental imbalance. Consistently, have one youngster in your group carry something that they might want to impart to the class. This won't just tell understudies with mental imbalance the best way to examine their inclinations with others yet in addition how to rehearse undivided attention. What's more, on the off chance that they're captivated by something one more understudy gets (or the other way around), they might try and make a companion.

3. Feeling Cards

These printable cards for understudies with chemical imbalance can assist them with figuring out how to perceive various feelings in themselves as well as other people. Remove everyone with scissors and mix them in a deck. Then, at that point, go through each card and check whether your understudy can perceive the feeling without checking the word out.

Assuming they stall out, that is OK — simply show them the word and give them a setting for the inclination shown. On the off chance that the card is "humiliated," for instance, you could say, "When an individual is humiliated, they could feel like they have accomplished something senseless or wrong coincidentally."

4. Prepackaged games with a Twist.

Showing youngster's habits can be a useful method for supporting interactive abilities and making sense of the significance of being well-mannered. This straightforward, yet successful action puts a decorum-related bend on a basic round of chess, checkers, or mancala by expecting players to wish their rival "best of luck" or "great game" when they have played.

5. How Would You Respond?

For a bring-back home movement you can impart to families, attempt this What Would You Do? game. Families can go through various situations together and conclude how they could respond with questions like "How might you help?" or "What might you say?"

This action keeps interactive abilities sharp and supports relationship-building abilities.

Tangible Activities for Children with Autism

Since youngsters with chemical imbalance are frequently hyper-mindful of tactile info, it's useful for teachers to give facilities so their understudies can concentrate in class. These exercises including tactile excitement can keep jokes with mental imbalance grounded in the present and open to learning with their other schoolmates.

6. Arranging with Snacks Activity.

This material action for youngsters with mental imbalance can be a pleasant method for drawing in understudies during math time. Give everybody in your group a portion of food that is not difficult to sort, such as chewy tidbits or little saltiness. Colorful tidbits are great, however, you can likewise involve food that comes in various shapes, surfaces, or sizes.

To start with, request that they sort the food by variety, shape, or another trademark. Then, utilize the snacks to show understudies essential number-related abilities like counting, adding, or deduction. Whenever they've embraced the idea you need to instruct, reward your understudies by allowing them to eat the tidbit.

7. Vegetable Paint Stamps.

This workmanship action for kids with chemical imbalance draws in contact and sight to keep understudies zeroed in on their task. Before class starts, cut cuts of vegetables like potatoes, cucumbers, or peppers. Hand out a couple of vegetable cuts to every kid alongside a cup of paint. Teach your understudies to plunge the lower part of the vegetable cut into the paint and afterward press it against a piece of paper.

As your understudies utilize these natively constructed stamps, they will establish lively plant connections with their paper. From that point, your understudies can either leave them as they are or finger paint to change them into unconventional craftsmanship.

8. Logical Slime Experiments.

Ooze isn't just a famous specialty for small kids yet, in addition, it's an extraordinary tactile movement for mental imbalance in class. There are a lot of basic ooze recipes online-look into your number one and have some good times making it with your understudies. You can involve this as a material workmanship movement if you'd like or as a science action for rudimentary understudies.

9. Squirm Toys.

Squirm toys are a notable tactile device for assisting kids with autism and other tangible handling problems to remain mentally collected and centered. Contingent upon your accessible assets, you can either stock your homeroom with a couple of squirm toys or make your very own portion.

'We Are Teachers' has ordered a rundown of eleven squirm toys you can make on a tight spending plan with your understudies. From works of art like twirly gigs to reused pipe cleaners or popsicle sticks, you're certain to find something valuable for your homeroom.

10. Hear-able Sensory Play

At the point when the expression "tangible play" comes up, visual or text-based exercises for the most part rung a bell first. Mental imbalance Adventures, nonetheless, recommends including exercises that include sound — with a couple of guides to kick you off:

- A game of seat juggling.
- Background noise.
- Simon Says.
- Clamor dropping earphones
- Beat instruments like shakcrs, downpour sticks, or drums
- Tangible Bin.

Tangible containers can be helpful for two reasons. To start with, they energize separated guidance or autonomous play — the two of which can have scholastic advantages for understudies. What's more, second, they're a direct and open tangible experience for understudies with mental imbalance.

Quieting Activities to Prevent Autism Meltdowns in class.

At the point when understudies with chemical imbalance are feeling overpowered, the extreme reaction that they feel might make them fail to keep a grip on their feelings. This is called a "chemical imbalance total implosion" and is not quite the same as when understudies without chemical imbalance carry on in class. While the best methodology for chemical imbalance complete implosions is to look for help from a school-trained professional, these quiet down exercises can serve to de-raise upsetting circumstances.

1. Establishing Techniques.

Establishing methods are intended to assist us with zeroing in on the present during unpleasant circumstances.

The following are a couple of establishing exercises for youngsters with ASD to attempt if they appear to be unsettled:

- Build up to ten or present the letter set as leisurely as possible.

- Pay attention to quieting music and focus on the various instruments.

- List five unique things that you can see around the room.

- Take a stab at extending straightforward yoga activities and spotlight how your body feels.

- Hold something material like a piece of mud or a plush toy.

For more seasoned understudies with a kid with ASD, you could likewise attempt care reflection. This can create a comparable result and assist kids with tuning into the present instead of getting snatched up by their feelings.

2. Understudy Retreat Zone.

At the point when an understudy with chemical imbalance is overpowered, giving them a spot where they can unwind and enjoy some time off from tangible feeling can once in a while go far. Assign an edge of your group as the "Understudy Retreat Zone" and fill it with tangible toys, picture books, agreeable seats, and quieting exercises that understudies with mental imbalance could do all alone.

Give each understudy access to your class and know that assuming they feel restless or pushed, they can constantly require a couple of moments to de-pressurize in the Student Retreat Zone. Like that, you don't need to single your understudy with mental imbalance out yet told them that it's a choice. If your understudy with mental imbalance seems like they could utilize some time away from class, you could likewise inquire as to whether they might want to peruse or deal with schoolwork in the library for some time.

3. Quiet Down Drawer.

Material toys can assist kids with autism to quiet down assuming that they're disturbed since their brains are so sensitive to tangible data. Assuming you have kids with autism in your group, fill a cabinet in your study hall with toys that could assist with killing overpowering feelings. At the point when your understudy appears to be focused on or experiences difficulty centering, give them a tangible toy or two to assist them with unwinding.

The following are a couple of thoughts for tangible toys to place in your "quiet down cabinet:"

- Play batter
- Squirm toys
- Stress balls
- Weighted covers
- Fragrance-based treatment pads

4. Shading

As per an accomplice article by The National Institute for Trauma and Loss in Children distributed by We Are Teachers, shading pages can be an extraordinary brain-body practice for quieting down and zeroing in on the present time and place.

Keep a couple of shading pages close by, and propose them as a quiet down movement when your understudies are overpowered. For a couple of free shading, pages to kick you off, look at this asset from Disney.

5. Quiet Down Cards.

On the off chance that your understudy with mental imbalance battles with quieting down in the wake of areas of strength for feeling, quiet down cards can be a useful asset. Each card has a supportive thought for quieting down after a distressing second. Furthermore, the creator notes they can likewise be valuable for youngsters with tension — an extraordinary asset for your homeroom to have.

6. Careful Breathing.

Care is a procedure that urges kids to keep their psyche in the present and manage awkward feelings. Assuming your understudy is battling to quiet down, have a go at watching this careful breathing video to assist them with recovering.

Chapter 6

Effective Teaching Strategies for Children with Autism.

At times, the gaining qualities of understudies with autism might vary from the remainder of your group. Be that as it may, fortunately, the right showing procedures and strategies can keep youngsters with ASD on target to complete the school areas of strength for the year.

Attempt these tips, instructive facilities, and assets for understudies with autism to assist them with learning ideas that could somehow be challenging for them to get a handle on.

1. Bring Special Interests Into Lesson Plans.

Numerous youngsters with mental imbalance have an obsession with specific points or exercises. Exploit what they're enthusiastic about and use it while training understudies with autism to assist them with centering in class. If a kid with chemical imbalance loves space, for instance, you could design several related tasks about including the planets in our Solar System.

2. Use Multisensory Learning.

Many children with mental imbalance are multisensory scholars and don't concentrate also when tasks just draw in one of their faculties. Prestigious researcher and mental imbalance advocate Dr. Sanctuary Grandin once said, "I used to think grown-ups communicated in an alternate language. I think in pictures. Words resemble a second language to me."

Therefore, illustrations that draw in a few detects like sight, hearing, and contact can make understudies with chemical imbalance more responsive in class. You could, for instance, show kids with autism how to peruse magnet letters or sing a devoted tune to find out about American history.

3. Attempt a SMART Goal Challenge.

If an understudy with autism is struggling with school, plunk down with them and pick a SMART objective to deal with for the following month or semester. Savvy objectives are a viable method for assisting kids with autism to arrive at their true capacity, and they are:

- Explicit
- Quantifiable
- Settled upon
- Significant
- Time-bound

Assume, for instance, that your understudy with autism is experiencing difficulty figuring out how to perceive feelings. You could make an objective with them to rehearse streak cards with feelings on them consistently for five minutes and for the understudy to perceive each card before the month's over. However long the SMART objective hits the models in general, it can assist your understudy with zeroing in on ways of gaining ground.

4. Give Clear Choices

As per teachers at the custom curriculum program of St Joseph's University, youngsters with mental imbalance might become overpowered when given such a large number of choices. Remember this while making tasks for your understudies or asking them inquiries in class. Like that, you're bound to keep your understudy with chemical imbalance engaged and open to picking a response.

5. Make a Strong Classroom Routine.

In an article with Scholastic, instructor Kim Greene reminds educators that understudies with chemical imbalance work best with areas of strength for a design. She proposes posting your class plan for each understudy to see and, if conceivable, giving visuals and additional progress time to understudies with mental imbalance.

6. Offer Accommodations for Students with Limited Motor Skills.

A few understudies with mental imbalance might experience more difficulty with exercises that require fine coordinated movements than others. In an article with the Indiana Resource Center for Autism, an eminent researcher and promoter Dr. Sanctuary Grandin proposes offering facilities — like composing on a PC as opposed to composing — to relieve these difficulties.

With regards to explicit facilities, it might rely upon the person. It's consistently really smart to connect with an understudy's family to decide the best assets for their youngster.

7. Exercises for Autism Awareness Month in April.

April is Autism Awareness Month when we praise neurodiversity and assist understudies with mental imbalance with feeling appreciated in private or state-funded schools. Although guardians may not believe their kid's chemical imbalance conclusion should be shared (and you never ought to without their consent), you can in any case show your class consideration this month without referencing a specific understudy.

Utilize these three beneath games as mental imbalance mindfulness exercises during April or at whatever point you need to show a thing or two on variety.

"Very much Like Me" Activity

For this action, assemble every one of your understudies on the floor so they can all see one another. Have every kid alternate sharing something important to them, such as:

"I have a pet canine."
"I can play the piano."
"My birthday is in September."
"I love to play soccer."
"My number one tone is yellow."

If an assertion likewise applies to different understudies (like, for instance, they additionally play the piano), educate them to lift their hands. This will assist with reminding understudies that they share a greater number of likenesses than contrasts with their friends and that they can constantly track down something to discuss.

Picture Books About Diversity.

By perusing a tale about comprehensiveness to your group, you can assist them with making sure to be thoughtful to everybody and post for unique individuals.

The following are a couple of picture books about the variety that you can impart to your understudies:

- The Sneetches and Other Stories by Dr. Seuss.

- I'm New Here by Anne Sibley O'Brian

- It's Okay to Be Different by Todd Parr.

- Wherever Babies by Susan Meyers and Marla Frazee.

- The Girl Who Thought In Pictures: The Story of Dr. Sanctuary Grandin by Julia Finley Mosca.

- The keep-going book on this rundown, The Girl Who Thought in Pictures, is about a renowned specialist who was determined to have mental imbalance and has since remained as a lobbyist for individuals with her condition. It is ideal for assisting jokes with understanding chemical imbalance somewhat better without getting down on a particular understudy.

Apples and Actions Game.
This practical example begins with showing your understudy an apple. Pass the apple around the class and, as you do, have every kid affront it and drop it directly in front of them or on the ground. After each youngster has dropped it and said something means to it, cut the apple down the middle and show your understudies every one of the injuries inside.

Clarify for them that our words have outcomes and that all that we say can affect another person. Very much like the way that annoying and dropping the apple can wound it, being spiteful to a cohort can immensely affect them. Like that, your understudies will constantly make sure to be thoughtful.

8. Autism Bulletin Board.

The unique piece is a well-known autism mindfulness image. For a straightforward yet significant method for showing your understudies chemical imbalance mindfulness, make this unique piece notice board from Mrs. D's Corner. Each piece battles against pessimistic generalizations by reminding your understudies that individuals with chemical imbalance are savvy, sympathetic, significant, and thus considerably more.

9. Show Students Historical Figures with Autism.

Albeit the issue wasn't found until the 20th 100 years, individuals with chemical imbalance have made significant commitments to history, and it's essential to teach understudies about them — in April as well as over time. The following are a couple of notable figures who are determined to have or accepted to have had chemical imbalance to kick you off:

- Greta Thunberg
- Vincent van Gogh
- Sanctuary Grandin
- Albert Einstein
- Emily Dickinson

10. Hold a Professional Development Session on Autism

It's so essential to show workforce mental imbalance mindfulness, as well. If you're a school head, think about holding an expert improvement meeting on showing understudies with mental imbalance or sharing a couple of assets.

Chapter 7

Embracing the new life.

Autism isn't consistently rainbows and daylight, however, it likewise isn't a misfortune. These 5 moves toward taking while embracing chemical imbalance are perfect and a must-peruse for guardians down and dirty who are battling with their kid's chemical imbalance.

Yet, in addition to the fact that it is critical to embrace chemical imbalance, in any event, when it's hard... It's practically more essential to embrace chemical imbalance when it's hard.

In any case, how would we do that? How would we embrace chemical imbalance when we're truly battling?

Before I bounce into these means... I simply need to require one moment to let you know that you are not a terrible parent.

Assuming that you're battling to embrace chemical imbalance today, that doesn't imply that you're a "fighter mother or father" or that you're hurting autistics and your youngster.

This is only a piece of nurturing.

Now and then it's difficult for me to embrace my child's talent. Some of the time it's difficult for me to embrace my little girl's cheekiness.

At times it's difficult to embrace raising young men and women.

Everybody has days when nurturing is difficult. The way that you're here perusing this post about how to return to a decent spot with your youngster's autism as opposed to posting negative things via virtual entertainment griping about your mentally unbalanced kid lets me know that you're a great parent.

With that far removed... How would we escape this funk and return to embracing mental imbalance?

- Recall That Your Child is Going Through a Hard Time, Not Giving You a Hard Time.

This appears to be messy, I know, yet this basic outlook shift will promptly help you to reconnect with your mentally unbalanced kid and recall that you're on a similar side.

It's hard when your kid is shouting in the supermarket.

It's considerably more enthusiastically to be a youngster crazy and overpowered at the supermarket.

Pause for a memorable minute that your kid isn't putting in to put forth your life more attempt.

Presently make it a stride further and recall that your kid's chemical imbalance isn't something that happens to you, it's a piece of what their identity is.

Very much like a kid being a kid isn't going on to you, it's a piece of what their identity is.

- Get some margin For Self-care.

Taking care of oneself is many times the keep going thing at the forefront of your thoughts when you're overpowered and battling to embrace chemical imbalance... I know.

- Search Out Extra Supports.

Commonly when guardians feel it's difficult to embrace mental imbalance this is because you're on this excursion alone (or it seems like it).

Perhaps your companion doesn't uphold the treatment meetings.

Perhaps your folks imagine that mental imbalance is a reason for an awful way of behaving.

Perhaps your companions don't come around any longer.

It all makes sense to me. I guarantee I do. I've managed an absence of help and it can feel genuinely dispiriting.

This is the point at which searching out additional supports is so significant.

Perhaps that looks like associating with different guardians of mentally unbalanced kids in Facebook gatherings.

Perhaps that looks like getting rest care through your state.

Perhaps that looks like having your life partner remove something from your plate, or employing a mother's assistant for one evening for seven days.

Whatever the arrangement, while you're battling to embrace chemical imbalance, now is the right time to get more help!

Vent in a Safe Space
Once in a while, you want to vent.

I vent constantly.

I have two explicit individuals who I vent on the standard:

Companion one and I are "go ballistic accomplices" for one another. We rate our concerns on a size of 1-10, and we give each other a clock. "You can blow a gasket for

seven minutes and 34 seconds." We are then allowed to vent, shout, cry, and freak out until our clock's up. When the clock is up, we must change gears and begin effectively fixing the issue.
Companion two, I can say "I couldn't care less assuming this is my shortcoming, I need NO rationale in this discussion". She then, at that point, knows that I'm going to vent and she must be my ally, regardless of anything. Whenever I'm finished, she assists me with really seeing the rationale, however not until I've vented bounty.
These companions both know and love me, AND know and love my children. So when I whine about my children, I realize they aren't taking that vent and utilizing it to frame convictions about my children.

As such, they're protected.

Presently, not every person has these companions. So what other place could you at any point track down a place of refuge to vent?

Shut. Private. Facebook gatherings.

Accentuation on private.

Find a gathering that is strong in chemical imbalance and neurodiversity.

You can make sense of your battle in a protected gathering and realize that the individuals in the gathering will assist you with clearing your psyche and understand what subsequent stages to take.

- Recall the Positives of Autism.

While you're battling to embrace chemical imbalance, I challenge you to take a couple of seconds to recall the upsides of chemical imbalance.

If you're truly dedicated, get some paper and record it on paper.

It needn't bother with to be extravagant... Just ponder what positive things have come from your youngster's chemical imbalance.

- Your youngster encounters bliss over things that others consider little and unimportant.
- Your youngster remembers EVERYTHING.
- Your kid's mental imbalance showed you the amount of a contender you could turn into.
- Your kid's mental imbalance assisted you with grasping neurodiversity and opened up another world to you.
- Your youngster finds things they love and embraces them completely.

- Your kid's autism showed you things yourself that you won't ever be aware of.

Those are models. Your youngster will have their assets and your excursion with chemical imbalance will have its positive sides.

Notwithstanding, carving out an opportunity to recall the advantages of autism will do ponders while you're battling to embrace mental imbalance.

www.ingramcontent.com/pod-product-compliance
Lightning Source LLC
LaVergne TN
LVHW050319160826
845677LV00014B/3471

* 9 7 9 8 8 4 8 2 2 7 8 6 4 *